GNARLY

A CHAPBOOK

DANIELLE SMITH

Copyright © 2015 Swimming with Elephants Publications

CONTENTS

*DISCLAIMER 7

CALCIUM CRUMBLE 8

MINERALS 10

PIÑATA 14

(HIS) TIE DYE 17

MEXICOLA 19

FRECKLES 21

SUPER 8 22

MAKING NOTHING OUT OF
SOMETHING 24

SELTZER SKY 25

GNARLY 26

ABOUT THE AUTHOR 30

GRATITUDE 30

*This is intended to be
an experience.*

*A messy,
personal,
brilliant
experience.*

*DISCLAIMER

The truth is,
I only want to love you from a distance.
I'm not good paddleboarding heart swells----
every time I've tried I end up
choking on salt water.

CALCIUM CRUMBLE

Bramble hands,
lion mane,
what a gorgeous destruction
she is.

Can't tell
heartache from toothache,
calcium crumble
like mortar to pestle;
she's gnarly.

Carbonated laughter
still bubbling inside after you
thought you'd forgotten
what it sounded like.

She's liquid sunshine,
eucalyptus,
too much voltage
not enough
shock absorption
always too much
too soon,
she's messy.

Misused skeleton keys,
barbed wire,
hiding under the bed
waiting to see if
the monsters will come,

cuddle up forehead to forehead
tell her
all about what scares them.

She's
heavy eyelids
sulfur stained finger prints,
waiting at the crossroads for
everything
to start falling into place.

MINERALS

I wanna compare
your eyes to mountains,
and it would make sense somehow
because some optimistic
hopeless romantic
would bend the rules of humanity
just to make my poorly
worded comparison
beautiful.

But see,
your eyes are nothing like mountains,
your eyes are minerals,
ground up and coughed out of hot springs.

I won't tell you I want to swim
in those sea green eyes,
because we both know,
I wanna soak in them.

Feel every white bit of skin
submerged in your swirling pools
reflecting my desert sun,
Your sacred mood – illuminating.
I could compare your lips
to train tracks, knowing full well
that if our tracks cross,
we're equally liable for
the resulting collision.

That being said,
I wanna travel the country guided
only by your half-smile half-smirk,
Learn what makes apple pie so American,
and why the Sox and the Yankees
can't just hug it out.

Your lips, cracked and rough are
where I stage my suicides
every Sunday night.

Hit by your train of thought,
speeding because you didn't go
to mass with your grandmother.
Your lips rust with age.
Let me tell you about the sharp
angle your jaw breaks into---
An angle that makes geometry
textbooks straighten up and
quit being so fucking obtuse.

I don't mean sharp like razor blades
or jagged cut diamonds,
I mean sharp like hairpin turns
on ski slopes, and sharpie stencils on brick walls.

Sharp like dress blues,
pressed and lint rolled,
whites bleached and buttons sewn tight.

Putting my fingers up to trace
every contour, chin to temple.
You undress,

leaving pencil shavings on the floor---
your jaw is sharp, darling.

I'd like to consider the abstract
concept of your shoulders.
The mountains
          and valleys
                    and twisting roads,
winding down to meet your fingertips.
Shoulders permanently indented
like postcards from backpacking across Europe,
embossed by phones tucked
between shoulder & ear.

I bet you can still hear
those conversations today ---
recite a grocery list from last June.
Your shoulders ease into arms
rough with rocky mountainsides climbed,

easy curves like lazy rivers run
slowly as if willed into flesh.
Palms pressed with the scent of mango
body wash and grease off a car
not worth investing in,

trickling down into fingers wrapped
around drumsticks tapping the cadence
of walking away.

This is not a love poem;
this is my perception of you.

Head to toe,
you're the most perfectly imperfect,
indefinitely beautiful person I've ever lived to know.

I've been studying your structure
since the first time
I went skinny dipping in your eyes.

PIÑATA

You created me.

I am the product of your two peeling hands,
the marriage of paste and newspaper.
I am your hollow beast.

You spent hours hunched over my rough,
cracked cast, meticulously smoothed
every jagged corner,
every fractured limb.

You built my skeleton with cracked
palms and arthritic fingers.

I was born into layers of brilliant
tissue paper wrappings,
bound together by rainbow fringe---

You grafted my mantle in the image of you.

I was your project----
Just the two of us together, your efforts kneaded into me.
I wanted to live up to your expectations so deeply.

When you gave life to me,
I was innocent.
I loved you more than anything.
When you finally stepped away,
wiped the sweat from your brow,
I was flawless.

My variegated mane windblown,
you made me so beautiful.

You filled my empty carcass with delicacies,
gifted me with smiles,
                    and love,
                              and sticky sweet candies.

How did I ever become so lucky? So blessed?

As you carried me on your shoulders,
the children grinned up at me
with purple tongues and sweaty fists,
waving at me.

My own celebration!

You strung me up high in your tree
so that everyone could see,
and I smiled so wide that I cracked some of my plaster---
                    I knew you loved me.

                    I KNEW you loved me, too.

But you let them start swinging.
You let them crack a baseball bat
into my sides, my sculpture,
over and over again.

You watched them club off my limbs,
and you laughed.
You smiled and watched as I

fell from my crown and collapsed,
crumbled at the grip of button fingers
greedy and hungry for my contents.

You never said a word as your masterpiece
went to rubble----
and I loved you.

I loved you as you whittled
newspaper into my body,
I loved you as I lay motionless,
watching the wind carry away my battered tresses.

You made me beautiful with
the purpose of destroying me,
and I loved you still
for the time you took to make me.

(HIS) TIE DYE

You call me late night sweater stains;
call me toothache and windowpane.
You call me Danger-Days,
caution tape---
You call me back-break.

I call you my Everyday Valentine.

Baby,
do you remember
when I called you mine?

Do you remember
those calico ink-spit
love letters I wrote to you
with a sock on my door,
and Ritalin in my heart?

Do you remember my callused,
lead heels hugging the floor,
sinking into one last goodnight?

Baby,
have you forgotten our
bone-crush pinkie-swears,
our cold pizza sunrise breakfast,
our sleepy eyes,
always too full of sand,
our barefoot backdoor banter---

You ran away from me yelling

'monster'
            yelling
                        'martyr'

calling me

            "Too much
            shag carpet,
            lava lamp,
            joystick"

            calling me stray cat---

Baby,
do you remember when we were 'Us'?

When I see you
wearing his tie-dye shirt,
I think you are wearing mine.

I hope you are wearing mine.

MEXICOLA

The desert sun was nodding off
when I knocked on the door.
I could already hear you dropping
accents like dinner plates.
Laughter shaking the drywall like an earthquake.

I shuffled through the doorway and soon after
found myself in the garage with a plastic cup of coke---
My Uncle Larry and Matthew swapping
mandolin string plucks.

I'm starting to allow myself to get comfortable.

Starting to notice the scent of limes,
salt, and new paint coating your halls.
Grandma is serving chile by the spoonful,
the kids are pocketing sweets for later tonight,
and I am on the roof,
feeling the agave breeze kiss my shoulders
looking out at that brilliant Duke City skyline.

I'd never been very well acquainted
with the land of enchantment
until I learned New Mexico through
my stepdad's enchiladas,
through my grandmothers red chile
and the way that my aunt Gloria speaks.
I learned heritage through my Uncle Gabe's accent,
through my cousins mariachi performances,
through my weekends spent on the ranch.

I'm sitting on the roof,
watching the sky blush every shade of ristra.
The horizon is a sea of twinkling lights,
a sea of angel kisses across Burque.
I can hear my family laughing and telling
loud happy stories in the backyard,

and New Mexico welcomes me home.

FRECKLES

Sometimes,
when you're not looking,
I pretend that your freckles are constellations.

I want to know the stories behind them,
remember them even through closed eyelids.

Sometimes,
I look up at you
and memorize the patterns across your nose.

They're the only directions I need
to find my way home.

SUPER 8

She

          stopped returning phone calls.
Her voicemail says she's not
home right now.

He's not home either.
He hasn't been home since she
stopped calling him 'Kid'.
There is an inescapable lowness in
becoming

Used To

          the silence in her wake.
He's checked in at the motel,
staring at his wishbone rabbit ear
TV antennas,
wrapping himself in sandpaper
sheets,
speculating that even the moldy
carpet might smell better
if she were there.
Wet curls and coconut shampoo,
she'd make this two-star motel

Feel

          like the Ritz;
but it's 4:49 AM and he's still
alone,
staring out of the window,
violent mind, violet sky
blinking slow and deliberate

Like

        faucet drips,
        cadence tapping insomniatic
        minute hand ticks.
        He didn't want to sleep, anyway.

        It is 10:16 AM,
        he is checking out of the motel,
        leaving her one more voicemail.
        Telling her that he misses her.
        Telling her that wherever she is,
        he hopes that she feels at

Home.

MAKING NOTHING OUT OF SOMETHING

Your fists do not
belong in my ribcage.
You take each exhalation
for vacancy in my lungs
as though you are entitled
to occupy the only space inside me
that I've learned to trust.

You call me "Dollface"
like you don't realize
porcelain can chip easily;
making nothing out of something,
as if my body wasn't enough for you.

**

You kiss me with eyes open,
pressing S.O.S into my shoulder blades
bloom black and blue cherry blossoms-
& I blame myself,
because everybody knows,
growing boys have
growing appetites.

SELTZER SKY

I remember the night
you woke me up
talking too quickly about the moon
bleeding something awful;
or the time you sat on the front porch
and waited for a meteor shower.
You said the universe was orchestrating
a grand firework show
just for us.

If I could have kept my
kindergarten eyes from sinking
dollar coins to the bottom
of a bubbling fountain,
I might have seen you sitting outside
telling this symphony of stars
all of your secrets.

Whispering things a sleeping
six year old girl
shouldn't know about her daddy.
Things best kept between
freckled face and seltzer sky.

GNARLY

Sometimes I feel like busted seems,
        this heartache isn't mine.
It just comes by sometimes,
kisses my forehead and leaves looking like

        iced coffee
        yucca
        pill bottles
        pill bottles
        pill bottles

I am mason jars and
chipped growlers full of
salt water and stars.
I'm too many 'I'm Sorry's',
goatheads in tangled hair,
I'm yours,
        I'm his,
                I'm afraid to be mine-
I can't think straight when you look at me like that.
I feel carsick.
You don't know that right now
I'm sitting behind you
writing this poem.
This shit poem, shit,
Maybe I should get back to my roots, live like

hot coffee
bare feet
ambulance
ambulance
ambulance

I'm lost and don't know my way home,
this filling on my tooth isn't me,
it's an extension of me
just like you are an extension of me.
Is it strange to say I don't think we've met yet?

Is it strange to say this is the most serious shit
I've written since I thought I needed to
take myself seriously?

Let's be honest here.
Maybe we're all just cardboard boxes
        (*open all the boxes*)
maybe we were never meant to be opened up.
Maybe we're just ugly teenagers
stuffed like pin cushions,
sprawled out on a horizon too blue to be true.
Maybe we're nothing.

cherry stem
cigarette
cigarette
gasoline

I'm scare to think of dying in an empty house.
I'm scared that I'll be chewing on
this pop rock rock bottom

until my ability to think pop-fizzles.
I'm scared that I'm always fighting a
losing battle with my brain---
I know that it fights dirty.

I'm scared of always being scared.

      locked doors
      fluorescent lights
      Daniel
      Daniel
      Daniel

This heartache isn't mine,
it belongs to you.
Here, let me help you with that.
Belongs to him, let me help put him back together.
Belongs to her, please, give me your
bad day, sad day, hate to be Alive day---
This isn't my heartache

      cold shower
      home alone
      vomit - panic
      vomit – panic

I don't know how to feel like myself,
Squeeze shut tsunami eyes,
disobedient dopamine,
Monsoon Mood swings----
This isn't my heartache.
This can't be my heartache.
I don't want this heartache.

                bedsheets
                voicemail
                taillights
                taillights
                taillights

I tiptoe across my perfect flat line horizon,
grinding teeth and popping knuckles,
I'm pressing palms into prayer hoping some day

                I'll understand what it means to be balanced.

ABOUT THE AUTHOR

Danielle Smith (Danny) is a 5'0" fiery, fiery firecracker. She lives in New Mexico and is a strong advocate for Mental Health Awareness. She enjoys bubbly beverages and swing dancing.

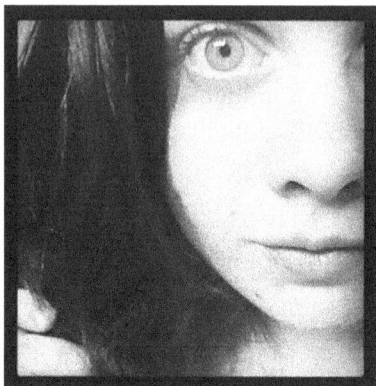

GRATITUDE

I feel so much love for the abundance of people who have been right by my side since the very beginning.

To my Friends, My life Preservers, Thank you for rejecting the concept of personal space. Thank you for just going with it. Thank you for letting me think that my bad jokes are funny. Thank you for being present.

To my Family, thank you for never turning your backs to me. Thank you for celebrating my successes as if they were yours. Thank you for being such a beautiful blended bunch of individuals with important stories to tell.

To Daniel, thank you for making everything less scary. Thanks for letting me feel human.

To Reed, thank you for rattling my brain with your poetry. It's been rattling ever since.

Oh Captain, My Captain, I cannot possibly repay you for all that you've done for me. You've read through countless drafts of poorly written poetry, talked me through many a heartache, you've shown me strength that I've never known in words. Thank you for being such an invaluable part of my life.

To My Parents: Thank you for every poetry club pick-up, every attended slam, thank you for listening to the same poem a million times over. Thank you for your unyielding support. I love you more than all of the angels lassoed together.

To Whomever May Be Reading This, Thank you. Thank you for every brave, compassionate, thought provoking thing you've ever done. Thank you for pausing to experience a piece of my journey.